Ripple Afghans

4

8

12

16

20

23

26

LEISURE ARTS, INC. • Little Rock, Arkansas

HOW IS THE RIPPLE PATTERN CREATED?

You will be amazed at the simplicity of the ripple pattern. We've broken it into 3 easy steps. Take a look –

1. MAKE THE CHAIN.

Ripple afghans, no matter how simple or intricate looking, begin with a beginning chain *(Fig. 1)*.

Fig. 1

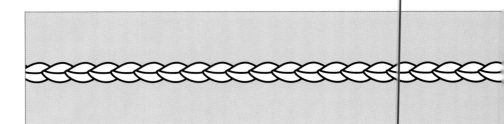

2. USE INCREASES AND DECREASES TO ESTABLISH THE PATTERN.

The first row starts the ripple pattern with evenly spaced increases and decreases. This creates the up and down pattern *(Fig. 2)*.

Fig. 2

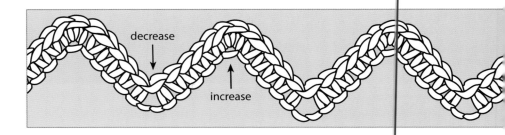

3. CONTINUE THE ESTABLISHED PATTERN TO CREATE THE RIPPLE.

Every row is the same with the increases and decreases "stacked" over each other, with the increases forming the "peaks" of the ripple and the decreases forming the "valleys" of the ripple *(Fig. 3)*.

Fig. 3

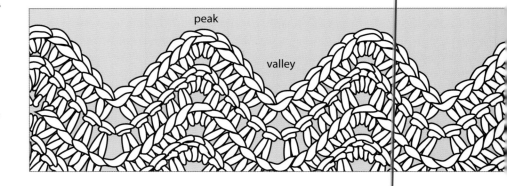

TRY IT YOURSELF!

Now that you have the concept, pick up some medium weight yarn and a size H (5 mm) crochet hook and try a swatch with a simple single crochet ripple. Please refer to General Instructions *(page 29)* for abbreviations and symbols & terms.

Chain 66 loosely.

Work Row 1: Sc in third ch from hook and in next 4 chs, 3 sc in next ch *(this creates the "peak" of the ripple)*, ★ sc in next 5 chs, skip next 2 chs *(this creates the "valley" of the ripple)*, sc in next 5 chs, 3 sc in next ch; repeat from ★ across to last 6 chs, sc in last 6 chs: 66 sc.

Work Rows 2-8: Ch 1, turn; working in Back Loops Only *(Fig. 10, page 30)*, skip first 2 sc, sc in next 5 sc, 3 sc in next sc ("peak"), ★ sc in next 5 sc, skip next 2 sc ("valley"), sc in next 5 sc, 3 sc in next sc; repeat from ★ across to last 6 sc, sc in last 6 sc: 66 sc.

Finish off.

🎥 HOW TO MEASURE RIPPLE AFGHANS

Because of the "peaks" and "valleys", ripple afghans and their gauge swatches are measured differently from typical rectangular afghans or swatches. Here's how to do it:

Lay your swatch or afghan on a flat, hard surface.

Measure one point-to-point repeat by placing the ruler from the center of one "peak" increase to the center of the next "peak" increase *(Fig. 4)*.

Measure the width from straight edge to straight edge.

Fig. 4

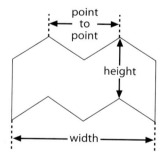

To measure the height of your ripple gauge swatch, place a ruler from the center stitch of a "peak" increase on the beginning ch to the highest point of the swatch *(Fig. 4)*.

For the length of your finished ripple afghan, measure from the bottom of the lowest point to the top of the highest "peak" *(Fig. 5)*.

Fig. 5

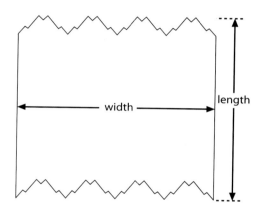

■■■□ **INTERMEDIATE**

Finished Size:

47" x 65" (119.5 cm x 165 cm)

SHOPPING LIST

Yarn (Medium Weight)

☐ Brown - 42 ounces, 2,040 yards
(1,190 grams, 1,865 meters)

☐ Green - 17 ounces, 825 yards
(480 grams, 754 meters)

Crochet Hook

☐ Size J (6 mm)
or size needed for gauge

GAUGE INFORMATION

In pattern, one point-to-point repeat
= 5¾" (14.5 cm);
8 rows = 4½" (11.5 cm)

Gauge Swatch:

11½"w x 4½"h (29.25 cm x 11.5 cm)
With Brown, ch 44.
Work same as Afghan Body Rows 1-8:
44 sts.
Finish off.

STITCH GUIDE

📹 **POPCORN** (uses one dc)

4 Dc in dc indicated, drop loop from hook, insert hook in first dc of 4-dc group, hook dropped loop and draw through st *(Fig. 6)*, ch 1 to close.

Fig. 6

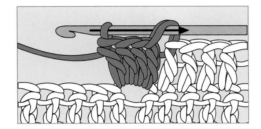

📹 **FRONT POST DOUBLE CROCHET** *(abbreviated FPdc)*

YO, insert hook from **front** to **back** around post of st indicated *(Fig. 12, page 31)*, YO and pull up a loop (3 loops on hook), (YO and draw through 2 loops on hook) twice.

📹 **BACK POST DOUBLE CROCHET** *(abbreviated BPdc)*

YO, insert hook from **back** to **front** around post of dc indicated *(Fig. 12, page 31)*, YO and pull up a loop (3 loops on hook), (YO and draw through 2 loops on hook) twice.

INSTRUCTIONS

With Brown, ch 170; place marker in third ch from hook for st placement.

Row 1: Dc in fifth ch from hook **(4 skipped chs count as first dc and one skipped ch)**, ch 1, dc in same st, [skip next 2 chs, (dc, ch 1, dc) in next ch] twice, skip next ch, 3 dc in next ch, skip next ch, (dc, ch 1, dc) in next ch, [skip next 2 chs, (dc, ch 1, dc) in next ch] twice, ★ skip next 4 chs, (dc, ch 1, dc) in next ch, [skip next 2 chs, (dc, ch 1, dc) in next ch] twice, skip next ch, 3 dc in next ch, skip next ch, (dc, ch 1, dc) in next ch, [skip next 2 chs, (dc, ch 1, dc) in next ch] twice; repeat from ★ across to last 2 chs, skip next ch, dc in last ch: 122 dc and 48 ch-1 sps.

Row 2 (Right side)**:** Ch 3 (**counts as first dc, now and throughout**), turn; (skip next dc, work Popcorn in next dc, ch 2) 3 times, work FPdc around next dc, dc in next dc, work FPdc around next dc, ch 2, work Popcorn in next dc, (ch 2, skip next dc, work Popcorn in next dc) twice, ★ skip next 2 dc, work Popcorn in next dc, ch 2, (skip next dc, work Popcorn in next dc, ch 2) twice, work FPdc around next dc, dc in next dc, work FPdc around next dc, ch 2, work Popcorn in next dc, (ch 2, skip next dc, work Popcorn in next dc) twice; repeat from ★ across to last 2 dc, skip next dc, dc in last dc: 74 sts and 48 ch-2 sps.

Row 3: Ch 3, turn; 3 dc in each of next 3 ch-2 sps, skip next FPdc, 3 dc in next dc, ★ 3 dc in each of next 6 ch-2 sps, skip next FPdc, 3 dc in next dc; repeat from ★ across to last 3 ch-2 sps, 3 dc in each of last 3 ch-2 sps, skip last Popcorn, dc in last dc 📷 changing to Green *(Fig. 13b, page 31)*: 170 dc.

Row 4: Ch 3, turn; skip next dc, (work BPdc around each of next 2 dc, work FPdc around next dc) 3 times, 3 dc in next dc, (work FPdc around next dc, work BPdc around each of next 2 dc) 3 times, ★ skip next 2 dc, (work BPdc around each of next 2 dc, work FPdc around next dc) 3 times, 3 dc in next dc, (work FPdc around next dc, work BPdc around each of next 2 dc) 3 times; repeat from ★ across to last 2 dc, skip next dc, dc in last dc.

Row 5: Ch 2 (**counts as first hdc**), turn; skip next BPdc, hdc in next 9 sts, 3 hdc in next dc, hdc in next 9 sts, ★ skip next 2 BPdc, hdc in next 9 sts, 3 hdc in next dc, hdc in next 9 sts; repeat from ★ across to last 2 sts, skip next BPdc, hdc in last dc.

Row 6: Ch 1, turn; working in 📷 Back Loops Only *(Fig. 10, page 30)*, sc in first hdc, skip next hdc, (work FPdc around FPdc one row **below** next hdc, skip next hdc, sc in next 2 hdc) 3 times, 3 sc in next hdc, sc in next 2 hdc, work FPdc around FPdc one row **below** next hdc, (skip next hdc, sc in next 2 hdc, work FPdc around FPdc one row below next hdc) twice, ★ skip next 3 hdc, (work FPdc around FPdc one row below next hdc, skip next hdc, sc in next 2 hdc) 3 times, 3 sc in next hdc, sc in next 2 hdc, work FPdc around FPdc one row **below** next hdc, (skip next hdc, sc in next 2 hdc, work FPdc around FPdc one row **below** next hdc) twice; repeat from ★ across to last 3 hdc, skip next 2 hdc, sc in last hdc 📷 changing to Brown *(Fig. 13a, page 31)*.

Row 7: Ch 3, turn; skip next FPdc, working in both loops, dc in next 9 sts, 3 dc in next sc, dc in next 9 sts, ★ skip next 2 FPdc, dc in next 9 sts, 3 dc in next sc, dc in next 9 sts; repeat from ★ across to last 2 sts, skip next FPdc, dc in last sc.

Row 8: Ch 3, turn; skip next dc, work FPdc around next dc, work BPdc around each of next 7 dc, work FPdc around next dc, 3 dc in next dc, work FPdc around next dc, work BPdc around each of next 7 dc, work FPdc around next dc, ★ skip next 2 dc, work FPdc around next dc, work BPdc around each of next 7 dc, work FPdc around next dc, 3 dc in next dc, work FPdc around next dc, work BPdc around each of next 7 dc, work FPdc around next dc; repeat from ★ across to last 2 dc, skip next dc, dc in last dc.

Row 9: Ch 3, turn; [skip next 2 sts, (dc, ch 1, dc) in next st] 3 times, skip next dc, 3 dc in next dc, skip next dc, (dc, ch 1, dc) in next FPdc, [skip next 2 sts, (dc, ch 1, dc) in next st] twice, ★ skip next 4 sts, (dc, ch 1, dc) in next BPdc, [skip next 2 sts, (dc, ch 1, dc) in next st] twice, skip next dc, 3 dc in next dc, skip next dc, (dc, ch 1, dc) in next FPdc, [skip next 2 sts, (dc, ch 1, dc) in next st] twice; repeat from ★ across to last 3 sts, skip next 2 sts, dc in last dc: 122 dc and 48 ch-1 sps.

Rows 10-114: Repeat Rows 2-9, 13 times; then repeat Row 2 once **more**; at end of Row 114, do **not** finish off.

Edging

Ch 4 (counts as first dc plus ch 1), do not turn; [dc, (ch 1, dc) twice] in top of last dc on Row 114; working in end of rows, skip first 2 rows, (dc, ch 1, dc) in each of next 2 rows, [skip next 2 rows, (dc, ch 1, dc) in each of next 6 rows] across to last 6 rows, skip next 2 rows, (dc, ch 1, dc) in each of next 3 rows, skip last row; working in free loops of beginning ch (Fig. 11, page 30), [dc, (ch 1, dc) 3 times] in marked ch, skip next ch, (dc, ch 1, dc) in next ch, [skip next 2 chs, (dc, ch 1, dc) in next ch] twice, skip next 3 chs, (dc, ch 1, dc) in next ch, [skip next 2 chs, (dc, ch 1, dc) in next ch] twice, ★ [dc, (ch 1, dc) 3 times] in next sp, (dc, ch 1, dc) in next ch, [skip next 2 chs, (dc, ch 1, dc) in next ch] twice, skip next 3 chs, (dc, ch 1, dc) in next ch, [skip next 2 chs, (dc, ch 1, dc) in next ch] twice; repeat from ★ across to last 2 chs, skip next ch, [dc, (ch 1, dc) 3 times] in last ch; working in end of rows, skip first row, (dc, ch 1, dc) in each of next 3 rows, [skip next 2 rows, (dc, ch 1, dc) in each of next 6 rows] across to last 6 rows, skip next 2 rows, (dc, ch 1, dc) in each of next 2 rows, skip last 2 rows; working in sts and sps across Row 114, [dc, (ch 1, dc) 3 times] in first dc, (dc, ch 1, dc) in each of next 3 ch-2 sps, skip next FPdc, [dc, (ch 1, dc) 3 times] in next dc, † (dc, ch 1, dc) in each of next 6 ch-2 sps, skip next FPdc, [dc, (ch 1, dc) 3 times] in next dc †; repeat from † to † across to last 3 ch-2 sps, (dc, ch 1, dc) in each of last 3 ch-2 sps; join with slip st to first dc, finish off.

Design by Barbara Shaffer.

DAISY BORDER

 **EASY +**

Finished Size:

45" x 62" (114.5 cm x 157.5 cm)

SHOPPING LIST

Yarn (Medium Weight)

- ☐ Variegated - 12½ ounces, 725 yards (360 grams, 663 meters)
- ☐ Ecru - 11½ ounces, 650 yards (330 grams, 594 meters)
- ☐ Green - 8½ ounces, 480 yards (240 grams, 439 meters)
- ☐ Brown - 7½ ounces, 425 yards (210 grams, 389 meters)
- ☐ Yellow - small amount

Crochet Hook

- ☐ Size G (4 mm)

  or size needed for gauge

Additional Supplies

- ☐ Yarn needle

GAUGE INFORMATION

Each Motif (from straight edge to straight edge) = 6¼" (16 cm);

In pattern, one point-to-point repeat (27 sts) = 6¼" (16 cm); 6 rows = 3" (7.5 cm)

Gauge Swatch:

6¼" (16 cm) (from straight edge to straight edge)

Work same as Motif.

STITCH GUIDE

▶ BEGINNING CLUSTER

(uses one st)

Ch 3, ★ YO twice, insert hook in **same** st as indicated, YO and pull up a loop, (YO and draw through 2 loops on hook) twice; repeat from ★ once **more**, YO and draw through all 3 loops on hook.

▶ CLUSTER (uses one sc)

★ YO twice, insert hook in sc indicated, YO and pull up a loop, (YO and draw through 2 loops on hook) twice; repeat from ★ 2 times **more**, YO and draw through all 4 loops on hook.

▶ SC DECREASE

Pull up a loop in each of next 2 dc, YO and draw through all 3 loops on hook (**counts as one** sc).

▶ DC DECREASE (uses next 2 sts)

★ YO, insert hook in **next** st, YO and pull up a loop, YO and draw through 2 loops on hook; repeat from ★ once **more**, YO and draw through all 3 loops on hook (**counts as one dc**).

INSTRUCTIONS

Motif (Make 7)

Rnd 1 (Right side): With Yellow, ch 2, 6 sc in second ch from hook; join with slip st to first sc, finish off.

Note: Loop a short piece of yarn around any stitch to mark Rnd 1 as **right** side.

Rnd 2: With **right** side facing, join Ecru with slip st in any sc; work (Beginning Cluster, ch 3, Cluster) in same st, ch 3, (work Cluster, ch 3) twice in each sc around; join with slip st to top of Beginning Cluster, finish off: 12 ch-3 sps.

Rnd 3: With **right** side facing, ▶ join Green with sc in any ch-3 sp *(Figs. 8a & b, page 30)*; ch 3, 3 dc in same sp, (sc, ch 3, 3 dc) in next ch-3 sp and in each ch-3 sp around; join with slip st to first sc.

Rnd 4: (Slip st, ch 1, sc) in first ch-3 sp, ch 5, (sc in next ch-3 sp, ch 5) around; join with slip st to first sc, finish off.

Rnd 5: With **right** side facing, 🎥 join Brown with dc in any ch-5 sp *(Fig. 8c, page 30)*; (2 dc, ch 3, 3 dc) in same sp, 5 dc in next ch-5 sp, ★ (3 dc, ch 3, 3 dc) in next ch-5 sp, 5 dc in next ch-5 sp; repeat from ★ around; join with slip st to first dc, finish off: 66 dc and 6 ch-3 sps.

Rnd 6: With **right** side facing, join Ecru with sc in any ch-3 sp; 2 sc in same sp, sc in next 11 dc, (3 sc in next ch-3 sp, sc in next 11 dc) around; join with slip st to first sc, finish off: 84 sc.

Assembly

With Ecru and 🎥 working through **both** loops, whipstitch *(Fig.14a, page 31)* Motifs together to form a strip, beginning in center sc of first corner 3-sc group and ending in center sc of next corner 3-sc group.

Bottom Ripple

Row 1: With **right** side of long edge facing and working in 🎥 Back Loops Only *(Fig. 10, page 30)*, join Variegated with dc in center sc of first corner 3-sc group; dc decrease, dc in next 11 sc, 3 dc in next sc, dc in next 11 sc, dc decrease, ★ skip next joining, dc decrease, dc in next 11 sc, 3 dc in next sc, dc in next 11 sc, dc decrease; repeat from ★ 5 times **more**, dc in next dc; finish off: 191 dc.

Row 2: With **right** side facing and working in both loops, join Variegated with dc in first dc; dc decrease, dc in next 11 dc, 3 dc in next dc, dc in next 11 dc, ★ dc decrease twice, dc in next 11 dc, 3 dc in next dc, dc in next 11 dc; repeat from ★ across to last 3 dc, dc decrease, dc in last dc; finish off.

Row 3: With **right** side facing, join Ecru with sc in first dc; sc decrease, sc in next 11 dc, 3 sc in next dc, sc in next 11 dc, ★ sc decrease twice, sc in next 11 dc, 3 sc in next dc, sc in next 11 dc; repeat from ★ across to last 3 dc, sc decrease, sc in last dc; finish off.

Row 4: With **right** side facing and working in Back Loops Only, join Green with dc in first sc; dc decrease, dc in next 11 sc, 3 dc in next sc, dc in next 11 sc, ★ dc decrease twice, dc in next 11 sc, 3 dc in next sc, dc in next 11 sc; repeat from ★ across to last 3 sc, dc decrease, dc in last sc; finish off.

Row 5: With **right** side facing and working in both loops, join Green with dc in first dc; dc decrease, dc in next 11 dc, 3 dc in next dc, dc in next 11 dc, ★ dc decrease twice, dc in next 11 dc, 3 dc in next dc, dc in next 11 dc; repeat from ★ across to last 3 dc, dc decrease, dc in last dc; finish off.

Top Ripple

Rows 1-5: Work same as Bottom Ripple: 191 dc.

Row 6: With **right** side facing, join Ecru with sc in first dc; sc decrease, sc in next 11 dc, 3 sc in next dc, sc in next 11 dc, ★ sc decrease twice, sc in next 11 dc, 3 sc in next dc, sc in next 11 dc; repeat from ★ across to last 3 dc, sc decrease, sc in last dc; finish off.

Row 7: With **right** side facing and working in Back Loops Only, join Variegated with dc in first sc; dc decrease, dc in next 11 sc, 3 dc in next sc, dc in next 11 sc, ★ dc decrease twice, dc in next 11 sc, 3 dc in next sc, dc in next 11 sc; repeat from ★ across to last 3 sc, dc decrease, dc in last sc; finish off.

Row 8: With **right** side facing and working in both loops, join Variegated with dc in first dc; dc decrease, dc in next 11 dc, 3 dc in next dc, dc in next 11 dc, ★ dc decrease twice, dc in next 11 dc, 3 dc in next dc, dc in next 11 dc; repeat from ★ across to last 3 dc, dc decrease, dc in last dc; finish off.

Row 9: Repeat Row 6.

Rows 10 and 11: With Brown, repeat Rows 7 and 8.

Row 12: Repeat Row 6.

Rows 13 and 14: Repeat Rows 7 and 8.

Row 15: Repeat Row 6.

Rows 16 and 17: With Green, repeat Rows 7 and 8.

Rows 18-101: Repeat Rows 6-17, 7 times.

Edging

Rnd 1: With **right** side facing, and working across Row 101 of Top Ripple, join Ecru with sc in first dc; 2 sc in same st, sc decrease, sc in next 11 dc, 3 sc in next dc, sc in next 11 dc, ★ sc decrease twice, sc in next 11 dc, 3 sc in next dc, sc in next 11 dc; repeat from ★ 5 times **more**, sc decrease, 3 sc in last dc; working across end of rows of Top Ripple, 2 sc in each of first 2 dc rows, (sc in next sc row, 2 sc in each of next 2 dc rows) across to Daisy Motif, sc in next 13 sc, working across end of rows of Bottom Ripple, 2 sc in each of next 2 dc rows, sc in next sc row, 2 sc in each of next 2 dc rows; working across Row 5 of Bottom Ripple, 3 sc in first dc, sc decrease, sc in next 11 dc, 3 sc in next dc, sc in next 11 dc, † sc decrease twice, sc in next 11 dc, 3 sc in next dc, sc in next 11 dc †; repeat from † to † 5 times **more**, sc decrease, 3 sc in last dc; working across end of rows, 2 sc in each of first 2 dc rows, sc in next sc row, 2 sc in each of next 2 dc rows, working across Daisy Motif, sc in next 13 sc, working across end of rows of Top Ripple, 2 sc in each of first 2 rows, (sc in next row, 2 sc in each of next 2 rows) across; join with slip st to first sc: 772 sc.

Rnd 2: Ch 1, sc in same st, (sc, ch 3, sc) in next sc, ★ sc in next sc, (sc, ch 3, sc) in next sc; repeat from ★ around; join with slip st to first sc, finish off.

Design by Pat Gibbons.

AMERICAN WAVES

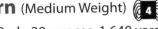

Finished Size:

46" x 60" (117 cm x 152.5 cm)

SHOPPING LIST

Yarn (Medium Weight) 🧶4🧶

- ☐ Red - 29 ounces, 1,640 yards (820 grams, 1,500 meters)
- ☐ White - 21½ ounces, 1,215 yards (610 grams, 1,111 meters)
- ☐ Blue - 4½ ounces, 255 yards (130 grams, 233 meters)

Crochet Hook

- ☐ Sizes G (4 mm) **and** H (5 mm) **or** sizes needed for gauge

Additional Supplies

- ☐ Yarn needle

GAUGE INSTRUCTIONS

Each Square = 3½" (9 cm);
In pattern, one point-to-point
   repeat (25 sts) = 4½" (11.5 cm);
   10 rows = 3¼" (8.25 cm);
   16 sc = 4" (10 cm)

Gauge Swatch #1:
   3½" (9 cm) square
Work same as Square.

Gauge Swatch #2:
   9"w x 3¼"h (22.75 cm x 8.25 cm)
With Red and using larger size hook,
ch 51.
Work same as Bottom Ripple, page 14,
for 10 rows: 50 sc.

INSTRUCTIONS
Star Strip (Make 2)
SQUARE (Make 19)

With White and using smaller size hook, ch 5; join with slip st to form a ring.

Rnd 1 (Right side)**:** Ch 1, 10 sc in ring; join with slip st to first sc.

Note: Loop a short piece of yarn around any stitch to mark Rnd 1 as **right** side.

Rnd 2: Ch 1, sc in same st, (2 dc, ch 5, 2 dc) in next sc, ★ sc in next sc, (2 dc, ch 5, 2 dc) in next sc; repeat from ★ around; join with slip st to first sc, finish off: 5 ch-5 sps.

Rnd 3: With **right** side facing and using smaller size hook, 🎥 join Blue with sc in center ch of any ch-5 *(Figs. 8a & b, page 30)*; ch 7, (sc in center ch of next ch-5, ch 7) around; join with slip st to first sc: 5 sc and 5 ch-7 sps.

Rnd 4: Ch 5 (**counts as first dc plus ch 2, now and throughout**), dc in same st and in next ch, hdc in next ch, sc in next 5 chs, hdc in next sc, dc in next ch, ★ (dc, ch 2, dc) in next ch, dc in next ch, hdc in next st, sc in next 5 sts, hdc in next ch, dc in next ch; repeat from ★ 2 times **more**; join with slip st to first dc, finish off: 44 sts and 4 ch-2 sps.

HALF SQUARE (Make 2)

With White and using smaller size hook, ch 5; join with slip st to form a ring.

Row 1: Ch 1, 6 sc in ring; do **not** join.

Row 2 (Right side)**:** Ch 3 (**counts as first dc**), turn; (dc, ch 5, 2 dc) in same st, sc in next sc, ★ (2 dc, ch 5, 2 dc) in next sc, sc in next sc; repeat from ★ once **more**; finish off: 3 ch-5 sps.

Note: Mark Row 2 as **right** side.

Row 3: With **wrong** side facing and using smaller size hook, join Blue with slip st in first sc; (ch 7, sc in center ch of next ch-5) 3 times, leave last 2 dc unworked: 3 sc and 3 ch-7 sps.

Row 4: Ch 5, turn; dc in same st and in next ch, † hdc in next ch, sc in next 5 sts, hdc in next st, dc in next ch, (dc, ch 2, dc) in next ch †, dc in next ch, repeat from † to † once, leave last 3 chs unworked; finish off: 24 sts and 3 ch-2 sps.

ASSEMBLY

With Blue, using Placement Diagram as a guide, and 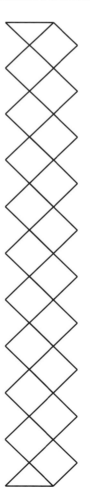 working through **inside** loops only, whipstitch *(Fig. 14b, page 31)* 19 Squares and 2 Half Squares together to form one Strip, beginning in second ch of first corner ch-2 and ending in first ch of next corner ch-2.

PLACEMENT DIAGRAM

TRIM

With **right** side facing and using larger size hook, skip first dc and next ch on first Half Square and join Red with sc in next ch; sc in next 11 sts, pull up a loop in next dc and in next ch, YO and draw through all 3 loops on hook, skip next joining, pull up a loop in next ch on next Square and in next dc, YO and draw through all 3 loops on hook, ★ sc in next 10 sts, 3 sc in next corner ch-2 sp, sc in next 10 sts, pull up a loop in next dc and in next ch, YO and draw through all 3 loops on hook, skip next joining, pull up a loop in next ch on next Square and in next dc, YO and draw through all 3 loops on hook; repeat from ★ 8 times **more**, sc in next 12 sts, leave last dc unworked; finish off: 251 sts.

Bottom Ripple

With Red and using larger size hook, ch 251.

Row 1 (Wrong side)**:** Sc in second ch from hook, skip next ch, sc in next 10 chs, 3 sc in next ch, ★ sc in next 11 chs, skip next 2 chs, sc in next 11 chs, 3 sc in next ch; repeat from ★ across to last 12 chs, sc in next 10 chs, skip next ch, sc in last ch: 250 sc.

Note: Mark the **back** of any stitch on Row 1 as **right** side and bottom edge.

Rows 2-10: Ch 1, turn; sc in both loops of first sc, skip next sc, working in 🎥 Back Loops Only *(Fig. 10, page 30)*, sc in next 10 sc, 3 sc in next sc, ★ sc in next 11 sc, skip next 2 sc, sc in next 11 sc, 3 sc in next sc; repeat from ★ across to last 12 sc, sc in next 10 sc, skip next sc, sc in **both** loops of last sc; at end of last row, finish off.

Row 11: With **wrong** side facing and using larger size hook, join White with sc in both loops of first sc; skip next sc, working in Back Loops Only, sc in next 10 sc, 3 sc in next sc, ★ sc in next 11 sc, skip next 2 sc, sc in next 11 sc, 3 sc in next sc; repeat from ★ across to last 12 sc, sc in next 10 sc, skip next sc, sc in **both** loops of last sc.

Rows 12-20: Repeat Rows 2-10.

Rows 21-30: With Red, repeat Rows 11-20.

Rows 31-49: Repeat Rows 11-29; at end of Row 49, finish off.

ASSEMBLY

With **right** sides facing, place Trim of one Star Strip adjacent to Row 49 of Bottom Ripple, matching stitches. With Red and working through **inside** loops only, whipstitch pieces together.

Center Ripple

Row 1: With **wrong** side facing, join Red with sc in corner sp at top of first Half Square on Star Border; skip next joining and next ch and dc on next Square, working in Back Loops Only, sc in next 10 sts, 3 sc in next ch-2 sp, ★ sc in next 10 sts, pull up a loop in next dc and in next ch, YO and draw through all 3 loops on hook, skip next joining, pull up a loop in next ch on next Square and in next dc, YO and draw through all 3 loops on hook, sc in next 10 sts, 3 sc in next ch-2 sp; repeat from ★ 8 times **more**, sc in next 10 sts, skip next dc, next ch, and next joining, sc in corner sp at top of next Half Square: 250 sts.

Rows 2-49: Work same as Bottom Ripple.

ASSEMBLY

With **right** sides facing, place Trim of remaining Star Strip adjacent to Row 49 of Center Ripple, matching stitches. With Red and working through **inside** loops only, whipstitch pieces together.

Top Ripple

Rows 1-41: Work same as Center Ripple.

Rows 42-50: Ch 1, turn; sc in both loops of first sc, skip next sc, working in Back Loops Only, sc in next 10 sc, 3 sc in next sc, ★ sc in next 11 sc, skip next 2 sc, sc in next 11 sc, 3 sc in next sc; repeat from ★ across to last 12 sc, sc in next 10 sc, skip next sc, sc in **both** loops of last sc; do **not** finish off.

Edging

Ch 1, do **not** turn; sc evenly across end of rows; working in 🎥 free loops *(Fig. 11, page 30)* and in sps across beginning ch, 3 sc in ch at base of first sc, sc in next 10 chs, ★ skip next ch, sc in next 11 chs, 3 sc in next sp, sc in next 11 chs; repeat from ★ 8 times **more**, skip next ch, sc in next 10 chs, skip next ch, 3 sc in last ch; 🎥 sc evenly across end of rows; working in **both** loops across Row 50 of Top Ripple, 3 sc in first sc, skip next sc, sc in next 10 sc, 3 sc in next sc, (sc in next 11 sc, skip next 2 sc, sc in next 11 sc, 3 sc in next sc) 9 times, sc in next 10 sc, skip next sc, 3 sc in last sc; join with slip st to first sc, finish off.

Design by Laurie Halama.

SIMPLE COMFORT

 **EASY**

Finished Size: 45" x 62½"

(114.5 cm x 159 cm)

SHOPPING LIST

Yarn (Medium Weight)

☐ Off-White - 14 ounces, 790 yards
(400 grams, 722 meters)

☐ Teal - 13½ ounces, 765 yards
(380 grams, 700 meters)

☐ Dk Teal - 13½ ounces, 765 yards
(380 grams, 700 meters)

Crochet Hook

☐ Size H (5 mm)
or size needed for gauge

GAUGE INFORMATION

In pattern, one point-to-point
repeat (14 sts) = 4½" (11.5 cm);
6 rows = 4¼" (10.75 cm)

Gauge Swatch:
9½"w x 3"h (24.25 cm x 7.5 cm)
With Off-White, ch 32.
Work same as Afghan Body, page 18,
for 4 rows: 27 tr and 2 ch-1 sps.

STITCH GUIDE

TREBLE CROCHET
(abbreviated tr)

YO twice, insert hook in dc indicated, YO and pull up a loop (4 loops on hook), (YO and draw through 2 loops on hook) 3 times.

FRONT POST DOUBLE TREBLE CROCHET *(abbreviated FPdtr)*

YO 3 times, insert hook from **front** to **back** around post of st indicated *(Fig. 12, page 31)*, YO and pull up a loop (5 loops on hook), (YO and draw through 2 loops on hook) 4 times.

DC DECREASE (uses next 3 tr)

YO, insert hook in next tr, YO and pull up a loop (3 loops on hook), YO and draw through 2 loops on hook, YO, skip next tr, insert hook in next tr, YO and pull up a loop, YO and draw through 2 loops on hook, YO and draw through all 3 loops on hook **(counts as one dc).**

ENDING DC DECREASE
(uses last 2 sts)

★ YO, insert hook in **next** st, YO and pull up a loop, YO and draw through 2 loops on hook; repeat from ★ once **more**, YO and draw through all 3 loops on hook **(counts as one dc).**

TR DECREASE (uses next 3 sts)

YO twice, insert hook in next dc, YO and pull up a loop (4 loops on hook), (YO and draw through 2 loops on hook) twice, YO twice, skip next st, insert hook in next dc, YO and pull up a loop, (YO and draw through 2 loops on hook) twice, YO and draw through all 3 loops on hook **(counts as one tr).**

ENDING TR DECREASE
(uses last 2 dc)

★ YO twice, insert hook in **next** dc, YO and pull up a loop, (YO and draw through 2 loops on hook) twice; repeat from ★ once **more**, YO and draw through all 3 loops on hook **(counts as one tr).**

INSTRUCTIONS

With Off-White, ch 160.

Row 1 (Right side): Dc in third ch from hook and in next 5 chs, 3 dc in next ch, dc in next 5 chs, ★ YO, insert hook in next ch, YO and pull up a loop, YO and draw through 2 loops on hook, (YO, skip next ch, insert hook in **next** ch, YO and pull up a loop, YO and draw through 2 loops on hook) twice, YO and draw through all 4 loops on hook, dc in next 5 chs, 3 dc in next ch, dc in next 5 chs; repeat from ★ across to last 2 chs, work ending dc decrease: 141 sts.

Note: Loop a short piece of yarn around any stitch to mark Row 1 as **right** side.

Row 2: Ch 3, turn; tr in next 6 dc, (tr, ch 1, tr) in next dc, tr in next 5 dc, ★ tr decrease, tr in next 5 dc, (tr, ch 1, tr) in next dc, tr in next 5 dc; repeat from ★ across to last 2 dc, work ending tr decrease; finish off: 131 tr and 10 ch-1 sps.

Row 3: With **right** side facing, join Teal with slip st in first tr; ch 2, dc in next 6 tr, work FPdtr around first dc of 3-dc group one row **below** next ch-1 sp, dc in next ch-1 sp on previous row, work FPdtr around third dc of same 3-dc group one row **below**, dc in next 5 tr on previous row, ★ dc decrease, dc in next 5 tr, work FPdtr around first dc of next 3-dc group one row **below** next ch-1 sp, dc in next ch-1 sp on previous row, work FPdtr around third dc of same 3-dc group one row **below**, dc in next 5 tr on previous row; repeat from ★ across to last 2 tr, work ending dc decrease: 121 dc and 20 FPdtr.

Row 4: Ch 3, turn; tr in next 6 sts, (tr, ch 1, tr) in next dc, tr in next 5 sts, ★ tr decrease, tr in next 5 sts, (tr, ch 1, tr) in next dc, tr in next 5 sts; repeat from ★ across to last 2 dc, work ending tr decrease; finish off: 131 tr and 10 ch-1 sps.

Row 5: With **right** side facing, join Dk Teal with slip st in first tr; ch 2, dc in next 6 tr, work FPdtr around next FPdtr one row **below** next ch-1 sp, dc in next ch-1 sp on previous row, work FPdtr around next FPdtr one row **below**, dc in next 5 tr on previous row, ★ dc decrease, dc in next 5 tr, work FPdtr around next FPdtr one row **below** next ch-1 sp, dc in next ch-1 sp on previous row, work FPdtr around next FPdtr one row **below**, dc in next 5 tr on previous row; repeat from ★ across to last 2 tr, work ending dc decrease: 121 dc and 20 FPdtr.

Row 6: Ch 3, turn; tr in next 6 sts, (tr, ch 1, tr) in next dc, tr in next 5 sts, ★ tr decrease, tr in next 5 sts, (tr, ch 1, tr) in next dc, tr in next 5 sts; repeat from ★ across to last 2 dc, work ending tr decrease; finish off: 131 tr and 10 ch-1 sps.

Rows 7 and 8: With Off-White, repeat Rows 5 and 6.

Rows 9 and 10: With Teal, repeat Rows 5 and 6.

Rows 11-86: Repeat Rows 5-10, 12 times; then repeat Rows 5-8 once **more**; at end of Row 86, do **not** finish off.

Trim
TOP
Ch 1, turn; sc in first 7 tr, (sc, ch 3, sc) in next ch-1 sp, ★ sc in next 6 tr, skip next tr, sc in next 6 tr, (sc, ch 3, sc) in next ch-1 sp; repeat from ★ across to last 7 tr, sc in last 7 tr; finish off.

BOTTOM
With **right** side facing and  working in free loops *(Fig. 11, page 30)* and in sps across beginning ch, join Off-White with sc in first ch *(Figs. 8a & b, page 30)*; sc in next 6 chs, ★ skip next ch, sc in next 6 chs and in next sp, (sc, ch 3, sc) in next ch, sc in next sp and in next 6 chs; repeat from ★ across to last 8 chs, skip next ch, sc in next 7 chs; finish off.

Design by Leanna Moon.

 **EASY**

Finished Size:

45" x 56" (114.5 cm x 142 cm)

SHOPPING LIST

Yarn (Medium Weight)

- ☐ Blue - 23 ounces, 1,390 yards (650 grams, 1,271 meters)
- ☐ Green - 20 ounces, 1,210 yards (570 grams, 1,106 meters)
- ☐ Variegated - 11 ounces, 665 yards (310 grams, 608 meters)

Crochet Hook

- ☐ Size I (5.5 mm)

  or size needed for gauge

GAUGE INFORMATION

In pattern, one point-to-point repeat (43 sts) and 23 rows = 7½" (19 cm)

Gauge Swatch:

4" (10 cm) square

With Blue, ch 17.

Row 1: Sc in second ch from hook and in each ch across: 16 sc.

Rows 2-20: Ch 1, turn; working in 🎥 Back Loops Only *(Fig. 10, page 30)*, sc in each sc across. Finish off.

STITCH GUIDE

🎥 **LOOP STITCH**

(abbreviated Loop St)

Insert hook in st indicated, wrap yarn around index finger of left hand 3 times, insert hook through all 3 strands on finger following direction indicated by arrow *(Fig. 7a)*, being careful to hook all strands *(Fig. 7b)*, draw through st pulling both loops to measure approximately 1" (2.5 cm), remove finger from loops, YO and draw through all 4 loops on hook *(Loop St made, Fig. 7c)*.

Fig. 7a

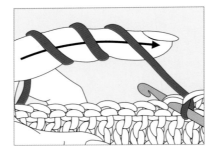

Fig. 7b

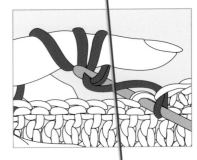

Fig. 7c

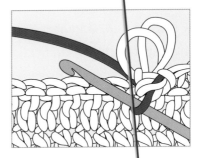

Afghan is reversible. You will have Loop Stitches on both sides of Afghan.

INSTRUCTIONS

With Blue, ch 263.

Row 1: Working in 🎥 back ridges of beginning ch *(Fig. 9, page 30)*, 2 sc in second ch from hook, ★ skip next 2 chs, sc in next 20 chs, 3 sc in next ch, sc in next 20 chs; repeat from ★ across to last 3 chs, skip next 2 chs, 2 sc in last ch: 262 sc.

Note: Before turning Row 1, loop a short piece of yarn around any stitch.

When joining a new color, the marker is used to indicate which side of the afghan needs to be facing. The Loop Stitch rows will alternate the side of the afghan that it's worked on.

Rows 2-10: Ch 1, turn; working in Back Loops Only *(Fig. 10, page 30)*, 2 sc in first sc, ★ skip next 2 sc, sc in next 20 sc, 3 sc in next sc, sc in next 20 sc; repeat from ★ across to last 3 sc, skip next 2 sc, 2 sc in last sc; at end of last row, finish off.

Row 11: With **marked** side facing and working in both loops, join Green with sc in first sc *(Figs. 8a & b, page 30)*; sc in same st, ★ skip next 2 sc, sc in next 20 sc, 3 sc in next sc, sc in next 20 sc; repeat from ★ across to last 3 sc, skip next 2 sc, 2 sc in last sc.

Rows 12-15: Ch 1, turn; 2 sc in first sc, ★ skip next 2 sc, sc in next 20 sc, 3 sc in next sc, sc in next 20 sc; repeat from ★ across to last 3 sc, skip next 2 sc, 2 sc in last sc; at end of last row, finish off.

Row 16: With **unmarked** side facing, join Variegated with sc in first sc; sc in same st, ★ skip next 2 sc, sc in next 20 sc, 3 sc in next sc, sc in next 20 sc; repeat from ★ across to last 3 sc, skip next 2 sc, 2 sc in last sc.

Row 17: Ch 1, turn; work 2 Loop Sts in first sc, ★ skip next 2 sc, work Loop St in next 20 sc, work 3 Loop Sts in next sc, work Loop St in next 20 sc; repeat from ★ across to last 3 sc, skip next 2 sc, work 2 Loop Sts in last sc.

Row 18: Ch 1, turn; 2 sc in first Loop St, ★ skip next 2 Loop Sts, sc in next 20 Loop Sts, 3 sc in next Loop St, sc in next 20 Loop Sts; repeat from ★ across to last 3 Loop Sts, skip next 2 Loop Sts, 2 sc in last Loop St; finish off.

Rows 19-23: Repeat Rows 11-15.

Row 24: With **unmarked** side facing, join Blue with sc in first sc; sc in same st, ★ skip next 2 sc, sc in next 20 sc, 3 sc in next sc, sc in next 20 sc; repeat from ★ across to last 3 sc, skip next 2 sc, 2 sc in last sc.

Rows 25-33: Ch 1, turn; working in Back Loops Only, 2 sc in first sc, ★ skip next 2 sc, sc in next 20 sc, 3 sc in next sc, sc in next 20 sc; repeat from ★ across to last 3 sc, skip next 2 sc, 2 sc in last sc; at end of last row, finish off.

Row 34: With **unmarked** side facing and working in both loops, join Green with sc in first sc; sc in same st, ★ skip next 2 sc, sc in next 20 sc, 3 sc in next sc, sc in next 20 sc; repeat from ★ across to last 3 sc, skip next 2 sc, 2 sc in last sc.

Rows 35-38: Ch 1, turn; 2 sc in first sc, ★ skip next 2 sc, sc in next 20 sc, 3 sc in next sc, sc in next 20 sc; repeat from ★ across to last 3 sc, skip next 2 sc, 2 sc in last sc; at end of last row, finish off.

Row 39: With **marked** side facing, join Variegated with sc in first sc; sc in same st, ★ skip next 2 sc, sc in next 20 sc, 3 sc in next sc, sc in next 20 sc; repeat from ★ across to last 3 sc, skip next 2 sc, 2 sc in last sc.

Rows 40 and 41: Repeat Rows 17 and 18.

Rows 42-46: Repeat Rows 34-38.

Row 47: With **marked** side facing, join Blue with sc in first sc; sc in same st, ★ skip next 2 sc, sc in next 20 sc, 3 sc in next sc, sc in next 20 sc; repeat from ★ across to last 3 sc, skip next 2 sc, 2 sc in last sc.

Rows 48-171: Repeat Rows 2-47 twice, then repeat Rows 2-33 once **more**.

Design by Joyce L. Rodriguez.

Shown on page 25.

 **EASY +**

Finished Size:
48½" x 68" (123 cm x 172.5 cm)

SHOPPING LIST

Yarn (Medium Weight)
☐ 46 ounces, 2,600 yards
   (1,310 grams, 2,377 meters)

Crochet Hook
☐ Size I (5.5 mm)
   or size needed for gauge

GAUGE INFORMATION

In pattern, one point-to-point
   repeat (14 sc and one ch-3 sp) =
   4" (10 cm); 5 rows = 2½" (6.25 cm)

Gauge Swatch:
7¼"w x 4"h (18.5 cm x 10 cm)
Ch 32.
Work same as Afghan Body for 8 rows:
28 sc and one ch-3 sp.
Finish off.

—— STITCH GUIDE ——

🎥 **DECREASE**
   (uses next 4 ch-3 sps)
★ YO, insert hook in **next** ch-3 sp,
YO and pull up a loop, YO and draw
through 2 loops on hook; repeat
from ★ 3 times **more**, YO and draw
through all 5 loops on hook.

INSTRUCTIONS

Ch 185; place marker in second ch
from hook for st placement.

Row 1: Working in 🎥 back ridges of
beginning ch *(Fig. 9, page 30)*, 2 sc in
second ch from hook, sc in next 5 chs,
skip next 2 chs, sc in next 5 chs, 2 sc
in next ch, ★ ch 3, skip next 3 chs, 2 sc
in next ch, sc in next 5 chs, skip next
2 chs, sc in next 5 chs, 2 sc in next
ch; repeat from ★ across: 154 sc and
10 ch-3 sps.

Row 2 (Right side)**:** Ch 1, turn;
working in 🎥 Back Loops Only
(Fig. 10, page 30), 2 sc in first sc, sc
in next 5 sc, skip next 2 sc, sc in next
5 sc, 2 sc in next sc, ★ ch 3, skip next
ch-3 sp, 2 sc in next sc, sc in next 5 sc,
skip next 2 sc, sc in next 5 sc, 2 sc in
next sc; repeat from ★ across.

Note: Loop a short piece of yarn
around any stitch to mark Row 2 as
right side.

Repeat Row 2 until Afghan Body
measures approximately 63"
(160 cm) from bottom of point,
ending by working a **wrong** side row;
do **not** finish off.

Edging

Rnd 1: Ch 1, turn; working in both loops, (sc, ch 3) twice in first sc, skip next 2 sc, sc in next sc, ch 3, skip next sc, sc in next sc, skip next 2 sc, sc in next sc, [(ch 3, skip next sc, sc in next sc) twice, (ch 3, sc) twice in next ch-3 sp, (ch 3, skip next sc, sc in next sc) 3 times, skip next 2 sc, sc in next sc] 10 times, ch 3, skip next sc, sc in next sc, ch 3, skip next 2 sc, (sc, ch 3) twice in last sc; skip first row, (sc in end of next row, ch 3, skip next row) across; working in ⬛ free loops *(Fig. 11, page 30)* and in sps across beginning ch, sc in marked ch, (ch 3, skip next ch, sc in next ch) twice, (ch 3, sc) twice in next sp, remove previous marker and place around last ch-3 made for st placement, ch 3, [(skip next ch, sc in next ch, ch 3) twice, sc in next sp, ch 3, skip next 2 chs, sc in next ch, ch 3, skip next ch, sc in next ch, ch 3, (sc, ch 3) twice in next sp] across to last 6 chs, (skip next ch, sc in next ch, ch 3) 3 times; skip first row, (sc in end of next row, ch 3, skip next row) across; join with slip st to first sc.

Rnd 2: Do **not** turn; (slip st, ch 5, dc) in first ch-3 sp, (ch 2, dc in same sp) 3 times, decrease, [(dc, ch 2, dc) in next ch-3 sp, dc in next ch-3 sp, (ch 2, dc in same sp) 3 times, (dc, ch 2, dc) in next ch-3 sp, decrease] 10 times, dc in next ch-3 sp, (ch 2, dc in same sp) 4 times, (dc, ch 2, dc) in each ch-3 sp across to marked ch-3 sp, dc in marked ch-3 sp, (ch 2, dc in same sp) 3 times, remove marker and place around center ch-2 of group just made for st placement, [(dc, ch 2, dc) in next ch-3 sp, decrease, (dc, ch 2, dc) in next ch-3 sp, dc in next ch-3 sp, (ch 2, dc in same sp) 3 times] 10 times, (dc, ch 2, dc) in each ch-3 sp across; join with slip st to third ch of beginning ch-5.

Rnd 3: (Slip st, ch 1, sc) in first ch-2 sp, ch 5, (sc, ch 5) twice in next ch-2 sp, [sc in next ch-2 sp, ch 5, sc in next 2 ch-2 sps, ch 5, sc in next ch-2 sp, ch 5, (sc, ch 5) twice in next ch-2 sp] 11 times, (sc in next ch-2 sp, ch 5) across to marked ch-2 sp, (sc, ch 5) twice in marked ch-2 sp, remove marker, [sc in next ch-2 sp, ch 5, sc in next 2 ch-2 sps, ch 5, sc in next ch-2 sp, ch 5, (sc, ch 5) twice in next ch-2 sp] 10 times, (sc in next ch-2 sp, ch 5) across; join with slip st to first sc.

Rnd 4: Slip st in first ch-5 sp, ch 1, (sc, ch 4, sc in fourth ch from hook, sc) in same sp and in each ch-5 sp around; join with slip st to first sc, finish off.

Design by Terry Kimbrough.

V-STITCH RIPPLE

 **EASY**

Finished Size:
45½" x 60" (115.5 cm x 152.5 cm)

SHOPPING LIST

Yarn (Super Bulky Weight)

- ☐ Black - 34 ounces, 600 yards
  (970 grams, 549 meters)
- ☐ Green - 13 ounces, 230 yards
  (370 grams, 210 meters)

Alternate colors:

- ☐ Lt Orange - 10 ounces, 176 yards
  (280 grams, 161 meters)
- ☐ Orange - 10 ounces, 176 yards
  (280 grams, 161 meters)
- ☐ Lt Green - 10 ounces, 176 yards
  (280 grams, 161 meters)
- ☐ Red - 10 ounces, 176 yards
  (280 grams, 161 meters)

Crochet Hook

- ☐ Size N (9 mm)
  or size needed for gauge

GAUGE INFORMATION

In pattern, one point-to-point
repeat (6 V-Sts and one dc) =
6½" (16.5 cm)

Gauge Swatch:
13"w x 4"h (33 cm x 10 cm)
Ch 48.
Work same as Afghan Body for 3 rows.

STITCH GUIDE

V-STITCH (abbreviated V-St)
(Dc, ch 1, dc) in st or sp indicated.

🎥 BEGINNING DECREASE

Make a slip knot on hook, YO, holding YO with index finger, insert hook in first dc, YO and pull up a loop (3 loops on hook), YO and draw through 2 loops on hook, YO, insert hook in next ch-1 sp, YO and pull up a loop, YO and draw through 2 loops on hook, YO and draw through all 3 loops on hook (**counts as one dc**).

🎥 DECREASE
(uses next 2 ch-1 sps)

† YO, insert hook in next V-St, YO and pull up loop, YO and draw through 2 loops on hook †, skip next 3 dc, repeat from † to † once, YO and draw through all 3 loops on hook (**counts as one dc**).

🎥 ENDING DECREASE

YO, insert hook in next V-St, YO and pull up a loop, YO and draw through 2 loops on hook, skip next dc, YO, insert hook in last dc, YO and pull up a loop, YO and draw through 2 loops on hook, YO and draw through all 3 loops on hook (**counts as one dc**).

🎥 PICOT

Ch 2, hdc in second ch from hook.

🎥 SC DECREASE

Pull up a loop in each of next 2 chs, YO and draw through all 3 loops on hook.

INSTRUCTIONS

With Black, ch 158; place marker in third ch from hook for st placement.

Row 1 (Wrong side): Dc in fifth ch from hook, (skip next 2 chs, work V-St in next ch) 3 times, ch 3, work V-St in next ch, (skip next 2 chs, work V-St in next ch) twice, ★ (skip next 2 chs, YO, insert hook in next ch, YO and pull up a loop, YO and draw through 2 loops on hook) twice, YO and draw through all 3 loops on hook (**counts as one dc**), (skip next 2 chs, work V-St in next ch) 3 times, ch 3, work V-St in next ch, (skip next 2 chs, work V-St in next ch) twice; repeat from ★ across to last 5 chs, skip next 2 chs, † YO, insert hook in next ch, YO and pull up a loop, YO and draw through 2 loops on hook †, skip next ch, repeat from † to † once, YO and draw through all 3 loops on hook (**counts as one dc**); finish off: 42 V-Sts and 8 dc.

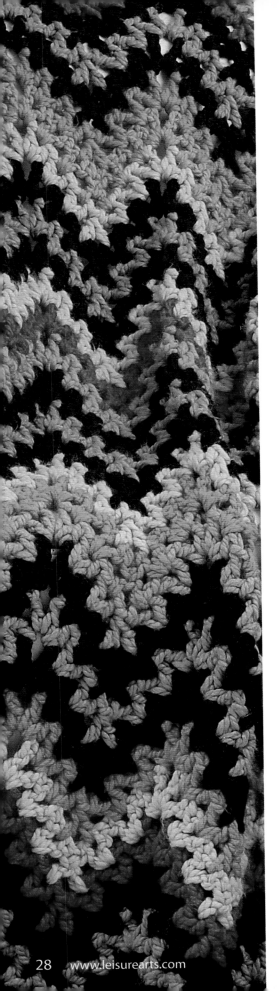

Note: Loop a short piece of yarn around **back** of any stitch on Row 1 to mark **right** side.

Row 2: With **right** side facing, join Green with beginning decrease, work V-St in next 2 V-Sts (ch-1 sps), work (V-St, ch 3, V-St) in next ch-3 sp, work V-St in next 2 V-Sts, ★ decrease, work V-St in next 2 V-Sts, work (V-St, ch 3, V-St) in next ch-3 sp, work V-St in next 2 V-Sts; repeat from ★ across to last V-St, work ending decrease; finish off.

Row 3: With **wrong** side facing, join Black with beginning decrease, work V-St in next 2 V-Sts, work (V-St, ch 3, V-St) in next ch-3 sp, work V-St in next 2 V-Sts, ★ decrease, work V-St in next 2 V-Sts, work (V-St, ch 3, V-St) in next ch-3 sp, work V-St in next 2 V-Sts; repeat from ★ across to last V-St, work ending decrease; finish off.

Note: Use alternate colors (Lt Orange, Orange, Lt Green, and Red) randomly throughout Rows 4-6.

Row 4: With an alternate color, repeat Row 2.

Row 5: With an alternate color, repeat Row 3.

Row 6: With an alternate color, repeat Row 2.

Row 7: Repeat Row 3.

Rows 8-44: Repeat Rows 2-7, 6 times; then repeat Row 2 once **more**.

Last Row: Repeat Row 3; do **not** finish off.

Edging

Ch 1, turn; sc in first dc, work Picot, (sc in next V-St, work Picot) 3 times, (sc, work Picot, sc) in next ch-3 sp, (work Picot, sc in next V-St) 3 times, † skip next dc, sc in next dc, (sc in next V-St, work Picot) 3 times, (sc, work Picot, sc) in next ch-3 sp, (work Picot, sc in next V-St) 3 times †; repeat from † to † across to last 2 dc, work Picot, skip next dc, (slip st, ch 2, dc) in last dc; working in end of rows, skip first row, (slip st, ch 2, dc) in top of dc on next row and each row across; working in free loops of beginning ch (*fig. 11, page 30)*, sc in marked dc, work Picot, sc in next sp, (work Picot, sc in next sp) 3 times, sc decrease, (sc in next sp, work Picot) 3 times, ★ (sc, work Picot, sc) in next sp, (work Picot, sc in next sp) 3 times, sc decrease, (sc in next sp, work Picot) 3 times; repeat from ★ across to last sp, sc in last sp, work Picot, (slip st, ch 2, dc) in ch at base of last dc; working in end of rows, (slip st, ch 2, dc) in top of dc on same row and each row across to last row, skip last row; join with slip st to first sc, finish off.

Design by Anne Halliday.

GENERAL INSTRUCTIONS

ABBREVIATIONS

BPdc	Back Post double crochet(s)
ch(s)	chain(s)
cm	centimeters
dc	double crochet(s)
FPdc	Front Post double crochet(s)
FPdtr	Front Post double treble crochet(s)
hdc	half double crochet(s)
mm	millimeters
Rnd(s)	Round(s)
sc	single crochet(s)
sp(s)	space(s)
st(s)	stitch(es)
tr	treble crochet(s)
YO	yarn over

SYMBOLS & TERMS

★ — work instructions following ★ as many **more** times as indicated in addition to the first time.

† to † — work all instructions from first † to second † **as many** times as specified.

( ) or [ ] — work enclosed instructions **as many** times as specified by the number immediately following **or** work all enclosed instructions in the stitch or space indicated **or** contains explanatory remarks.

colon (:) — the number(s) given after a colon at the end of a row or round denote(s) the number of stitches or spaces you should have on that row or round.

GAUGE

Exact gauge is **essential** for proper size. Before beginning your Afghan, make the sample swatch given in the individual instructions in the yarn and hook specified. After completing the swatch, measure it, counting your stitches and rows or rounds carefully. If your swatch is larger or smaller than specified, **make another, changing hook size to get the correct gauge.** Keep trying until you find the size hook that will give you the specified gauge.

ALUMINUM CROCHET HOOKS

UNITED STATES	METRIC (mm)
B-1	2.25
C-2	2.75
D-3	3.25
E-4	3.5
F-5	3.75
G-6	4
H-8	5
I-9	5.5
J-10	6
K-10 ½	6.5
N-13	9
P-15	10
Q-19	15

CROCHET TERMINOLOGY

UNITED STATES		INTERNATIONAL
slip stitch (slip st)	=	single crochet (sc)
single crochet (sc)	=	double crochet (dc)
half double crochet (hdc)	=	half treble crochet (htr)
double crochet (dc)	=	treble crochet(tr)
treble crochet (tr)	=	double treble crochet (dtr)
double treble crochet (dtr)	=	triple treble crochet (ttr)
triple treble crochet (tr tr)	=	quadruple treble crochet (qtr)
skip	=	miss

Yarn Weight Symbol & Names	LACE 0	SUPER FINE 1	FINE 2	LIGHT 3	MEDIUM 4	BULKY 5	SUPER BULKY 6
Type of Yarns in Category	Fingering, 10-count crochet thread	Sock, Fingering Baby	Sport, Baby	DK, Light Worsted	Worsted, Afghan, Aran	Chunky, Craft, Rug	Bulky, Roving
Crochet Gauge* Ranges in Single Crochet to 4" (10 cm)	32-42 double crochets**	21-32 sts	16-20 sts	12-17 sts	11-14 sts	8-11 sts	5-9 sts
Advised Hook Size Range	Steel*** 6,7,8 Regular hook B-1	B-1 to E-4	E-4 to 7	7 to I-9	I-9 to K-10.5	K-10.5 to M-13	M-13 and larger

*GUIDELINES ONLY: The chart above reflects the most commonly used gauges and hook sizes for specific yarn categories.

** Lace weight yarns are usually crocheted on larger-size hooks to create lacy openwork patterns. Accordingly, a gauge range is difficult to determine. Always follow the gauge stated in your pattern.

JOINING WITH SC OR DC

When instructed to **join with sc**, begin with a slip knot on hook. Insert hook in stitch or space indicated, YO and pull up a loop, YO and draw through both loops on hook (*Figs. 8a & b*).

Fig. 8a

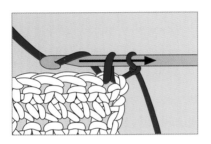

Fig. 8b

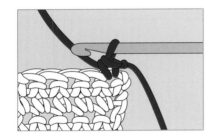

When instructed to **join with dc**, begin with a slip knot on hook. YO, holding loop on hook, insert hook in stitch or space indicated, YO and pull up a loop (3 loops on hook), (YO and draw through 2 loops on hook) twice (*Fig. 8c*).

Fig. 8c

BACK RIDGES

Work only in loops indicated by arrows (*Fig. 9*).

Fig. 9

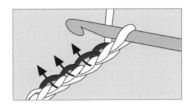

BACK LOOP ONLY

Work only in loop(s) indicated by arrow (*Fig. 10*).

Fig. 10

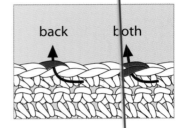

FREE LOOPS OF A CHAIN

When instructed to work in free loops of a chain, work in loop indicated by arrow (*Fig. 11*).

Fig. 11

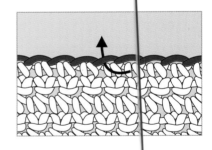

◼☐☐☐ **BEGINNER**		Projects for first-time crocheters using basic stitches. Minimal shaping.
◼◼☐☐ **EASY**		Projects using yarn with basic stitches, repetitive stitch patterns, simple color changes, and simple shaping and finishing.
◼◼◼☐ **INTERMEDIATE**		Projects using a variety of techniques, such as basic lace patterns or color patterns, mid-level shaping and finishing.
◼◼◼◼ **EXPERIENCED**		Projects with intricate stitch patterns, techniques and dimension, such as non-repeating patterns, multi-color techniques, fine threads, small hooks, detailed shaping and refined finishing.

POST STITCH

Work around post of stitch indicated, inserting hook in direction of arrow (Fig. 12).

Fig. 12

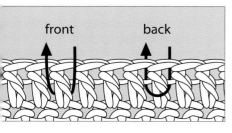

CHANGING COLORS

Work the last stitch to within one step of completion, hook new yarn *(Figs. 13a &b)* and draw through all loops on hook. Cut old yarn and work over both ends unless otherwise indicated.

Fig. 13a

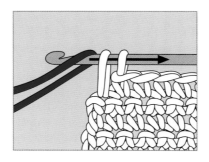

Fig. 13b

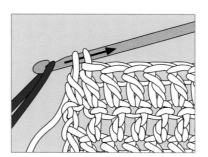

WHIPSTITCH

Place two Strips, Squares, or Motifs with **wrong** sides together. Sew through both pieces once to secure the beginning of the seam, leaving an ample yarn end to weave in later. Insert the needle from front to back through **both** loops on both pieces *(Fig. 14a)* or through **inside** loop only of each stitch on both pieces *(Fig. 14b)*. Bring the needle around and insert it from front to back through the next loops of both pieces. Continue in this manner across to corner, keeping the sewing yarn fairly loose.

Fig. 14a

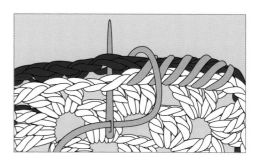

Fig. 14b

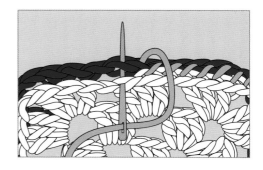

YARN INFORMATION

The Afghans in this leaflet were made using Medium Weight or Super Bulky Weight Yarn. Any brand of yarn in the specified weight may be used. It is best to refer to the yardage/meters when determining how many balls or skeins to purchase. Remember, to arrive at the finished size, it is the GAUGE/TENSION that is most important, not the brand of yarn.

For your convenience, listed below are the specific yarns used to create our photography models.

HILL & VALLEY
Lion Brand® Vanna's Choice®
Brown - #124 Toffee
Lion Brand® Vanna's Choice®
Baby Green - #169 Sweet
Pea

AMERICAN WAVES
Red Heart® Classic®
Red - #0914 Country Red
Red Heart® Super Saver®
White - #0311 White
Blue - #0387 Soft Navy

VIBRANCE
Red Heart® Kids™
Blue - #2845 Blue
Green - #2652 Lime
Variegated - #2940 Beach
multi

V-STITCH RIPPLE
Lion Brand® Wool-Ease®
Thick & Quick®
Black - #153 Black
Green - #132 Lemongrass
Lt Orange - #189
Butterscotch
Orange - #133 Pumpkin
Lt Green - #134 Citron
Red - #138 Cranberry

DAISY BORDER
Red Heart® Super Saver®
Variegated - #0305 Aspen
Print
Ecru - #0313 Aran
Green - #0631 Lt Sage
Brown - #0336 Warm Brown
Yellow - #0320 Cornmeal

SIMPLE COMFORT
Red Heart® Classic®
Off-White - #0003 Off-White
Teal - #0355 Lt Teal
Dk Teal - #0513 Parakeet

VINTAGE LACE
Red Heart ® Super Saver®
#0313 Aran

We have made every effort to ensure that these instructions are accurate and complete. We cannot, however, be responsible for human error, typographical mistakes, or variations in individual work.

Production Team: Writer/Technical Editors - Cathy Hardy and Susan Wiles; Editorial Writer - Susan McManus Johnson; Senior Graphic Artist - Lora Puls; Graphic Artists - Becca Snider and Dana Vaughn; Photo Sylist - Sondra Daniel; and Photographer - Ken West.

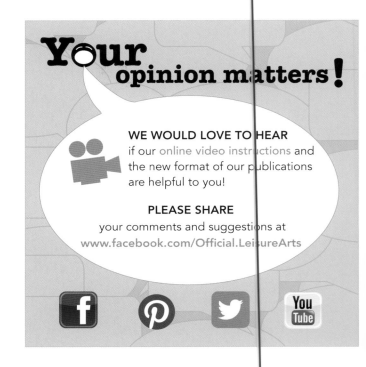

Your opinion matters!

WE WOULD LOVE TO HEAR if our online video instructions and the new format of our publications are helpful to you!

PLEASE SHARE
your comments and suggestions at
www.facebook.com/Official.LeisureArts